LAUGH WITH ME

ALL PHOTOS USED IN THIS PUBLICATION ARE FROM CANVA.COM. LISTED BELOW IN ORDER OF APPEARANCE

COVER: LAUGHING KID ON GREY BACKGROUND BY JNEMCHINOVA FROM GETTY IMAGES

LITTLE HANDLE NEWBORN BABY IN MOM'S BIG HAND BY CHAUNPIS FROM GETTY IMAGES

HAPPY KID BY GRANDPIX FROM GETTY IMAGES

LAUGHING BABY BY PIXLAND FROM PHOTO IMAGES

BABY LAUGHING BY NIKOLAYK FROM GETTY IMAGES

BABY INDOORS LAUGHING BY MONKEY BUSINESS IMAGES

LAUGHING BABY BY JUPITERIMAGES FROM PHOTO IMAGES

MOTHER AND CHILDREN BY VALERIA USHAKOVA COLLECTION

CUTE BABY LAUGHING I CRIB BY ARTEM VARNITSIN

BABY IS EATING BABY FOOD BY PINSTOCK FROM GETTY IMAGES SIGNATURE

BAD MOOD JAPANESE LITTLE GIRL BY DEEEPBLUE FROM GETTY IMAGES

CUTE CHILD LAUGHING BY PUWADON SANGNGERN'S IMAGES

YOUNG KID LAUGHING BY DIGITALSKILLET FROM GETTY IMAGES SIGNATURE

CUTE BLACK KID LAUGHING WHILE PLAYING WITH FATHER BY KETUT SUBIYANTO FROM PEXELS

LAUGHING KIDS BY KATE_SEPT2004 FROM GETTY IMAGES

SMILING KIDS IN THE SCHOOL BY ROBERTOVI FROM PIXABAY

KIDS AT THE BEACH BY FATCAMERA FROM GETTY IMAGES SIGNATURE

LAUGHING KIDS ON SWIMMING POOL BY WEEKEND IMAGES INC. FROM GETTY IMAGES SIGNATURE

BROTHER JUMPING ON BED WITH SISTER BY RODNAE PRODUCTIONS FROM PEXELS

SAD KID BY INDIANEYE FROM GETTY IMAGES SIGNATURE

LAUGHING CHLDREN BY FATCAMERA FROM GETTY IMAGES SIGNATURE

TWO LITTLE LAUGHING KIDS GIRLS OUTDOORS BY INDUSTRIAL PHOTOGRAPH

PORTRAIT OF TWO BOYS EMBRACING AD LAUGHING HARD OUTDOORS BY MONKEY BUSINESS IMAGES

KIDS PLAYING BY FATCAMERA FROM GETTY IMAGES SIGNATURE

LAUGHING KID BY NICOLESY

*HAPPY KIDS BY FATCAMERA FROM GETTY IMAGES SIGNATURE

- * IMAGE ALSO USED ON REAR COVER OF BOOK

LAUGH WITH ME

by Seneca Mahoney

Laugh With Me

Copyright © 2023 by Seneca Mahoney

All Rights Reserved

This book or any portion thereof may not be reproduced or used in any manner whatsoever without the express written permission of the author , except for the use of brief quotations in a book review.

Printed in the United States of America

IISBN- 979-8369754894

For Arius, Ailani and Ogechi. I'm so grateful for each one of you and I love laughing with you!

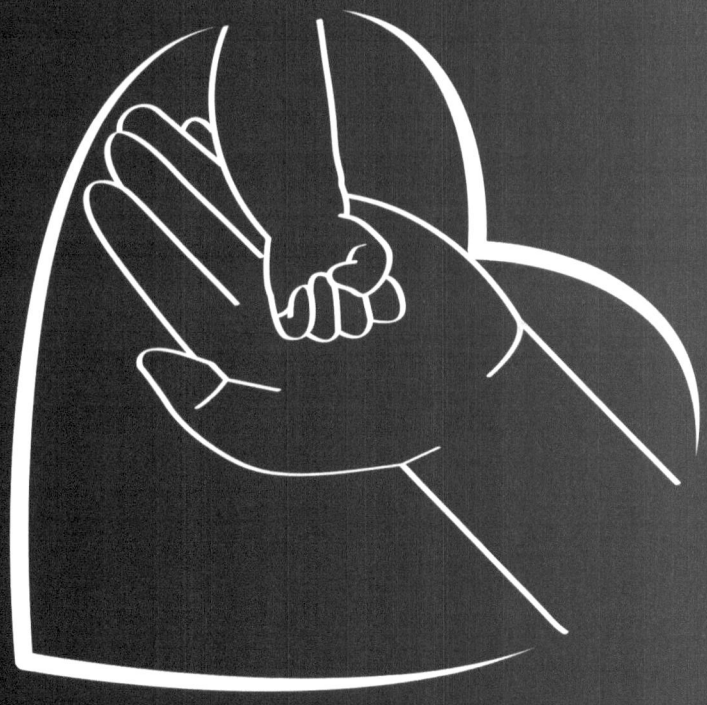

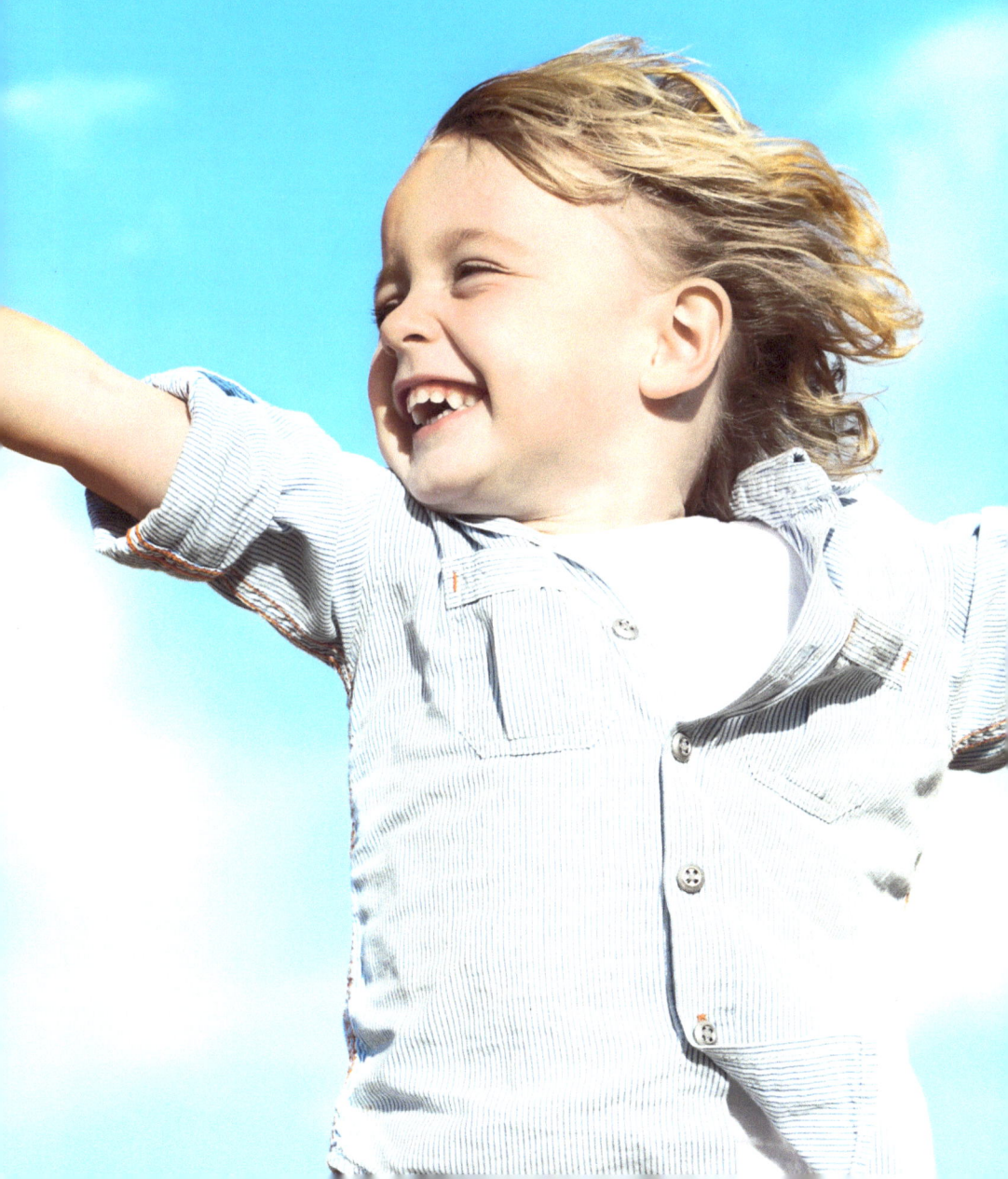

I love to laugh, I do it every day!

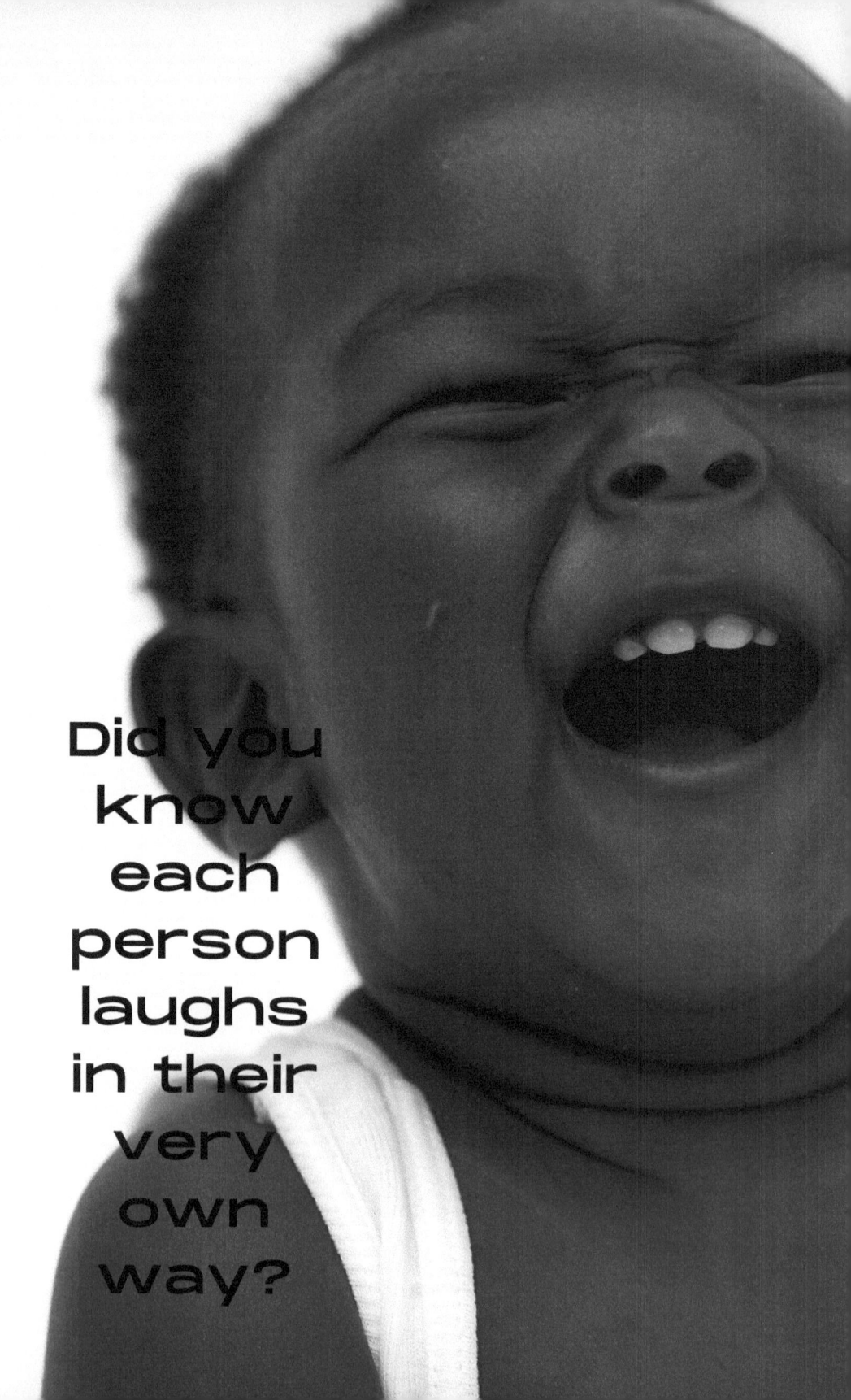

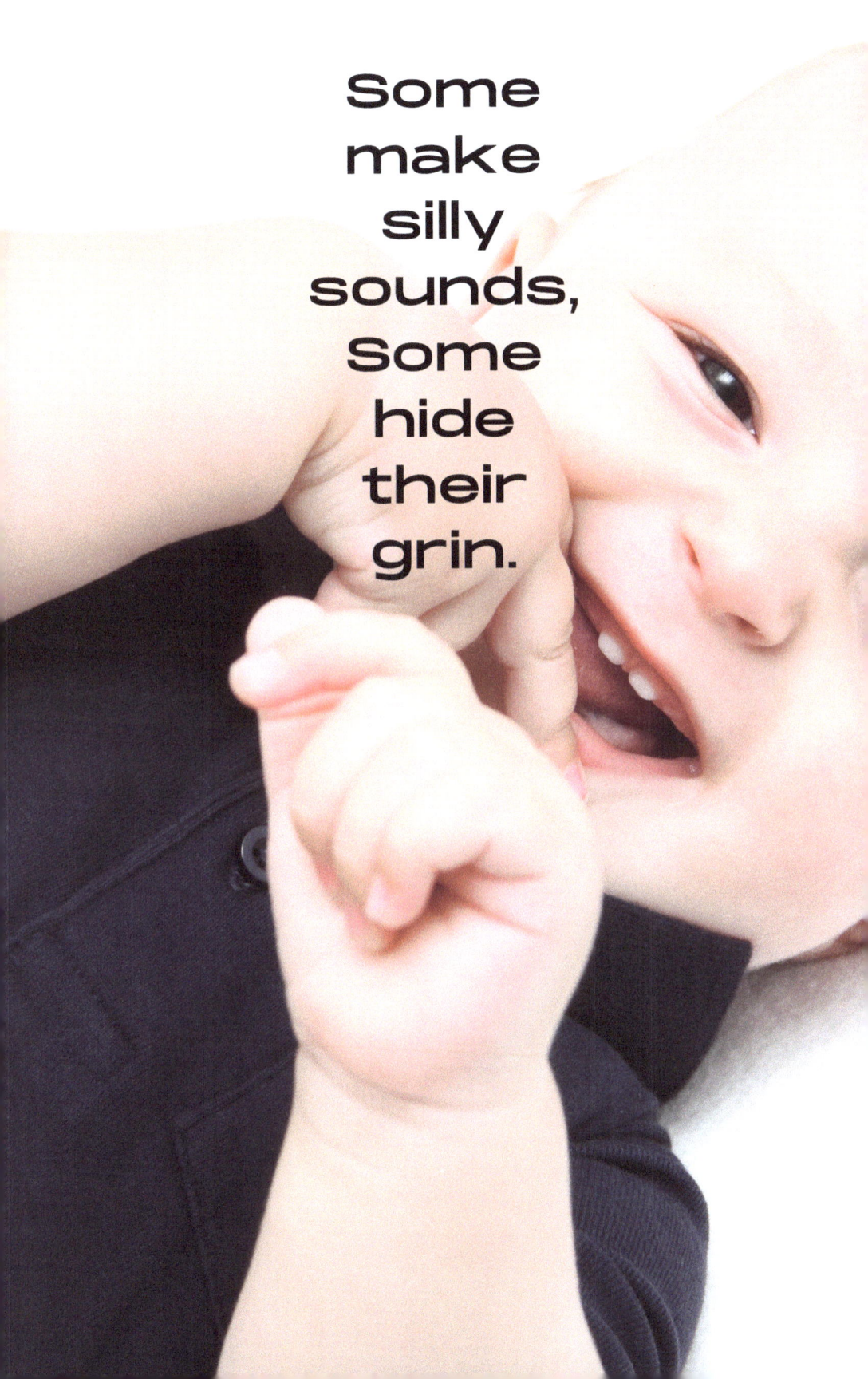
Some make silly sounds, Some hide their grin.

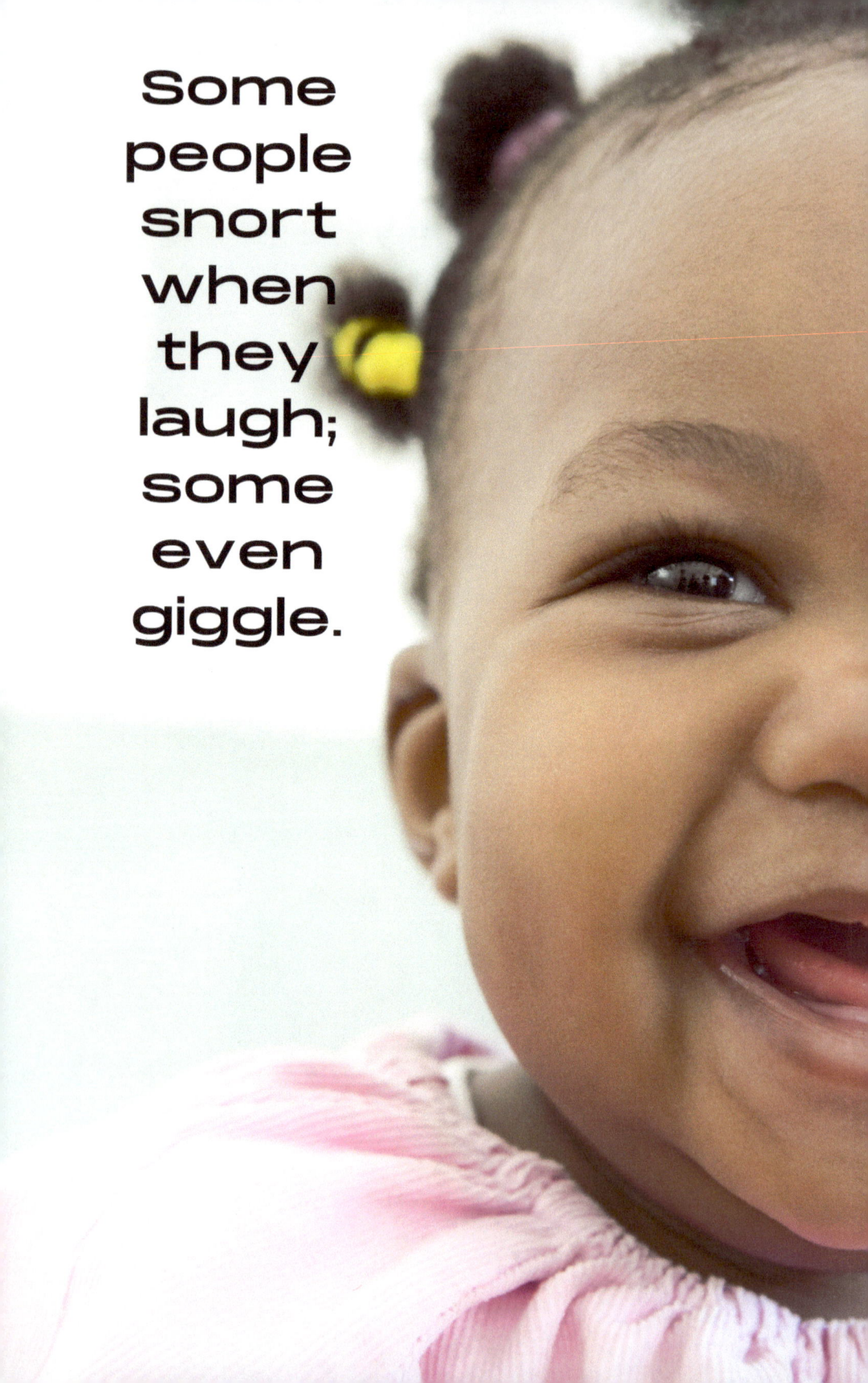

Some people snort when they laugh; some even giggle.

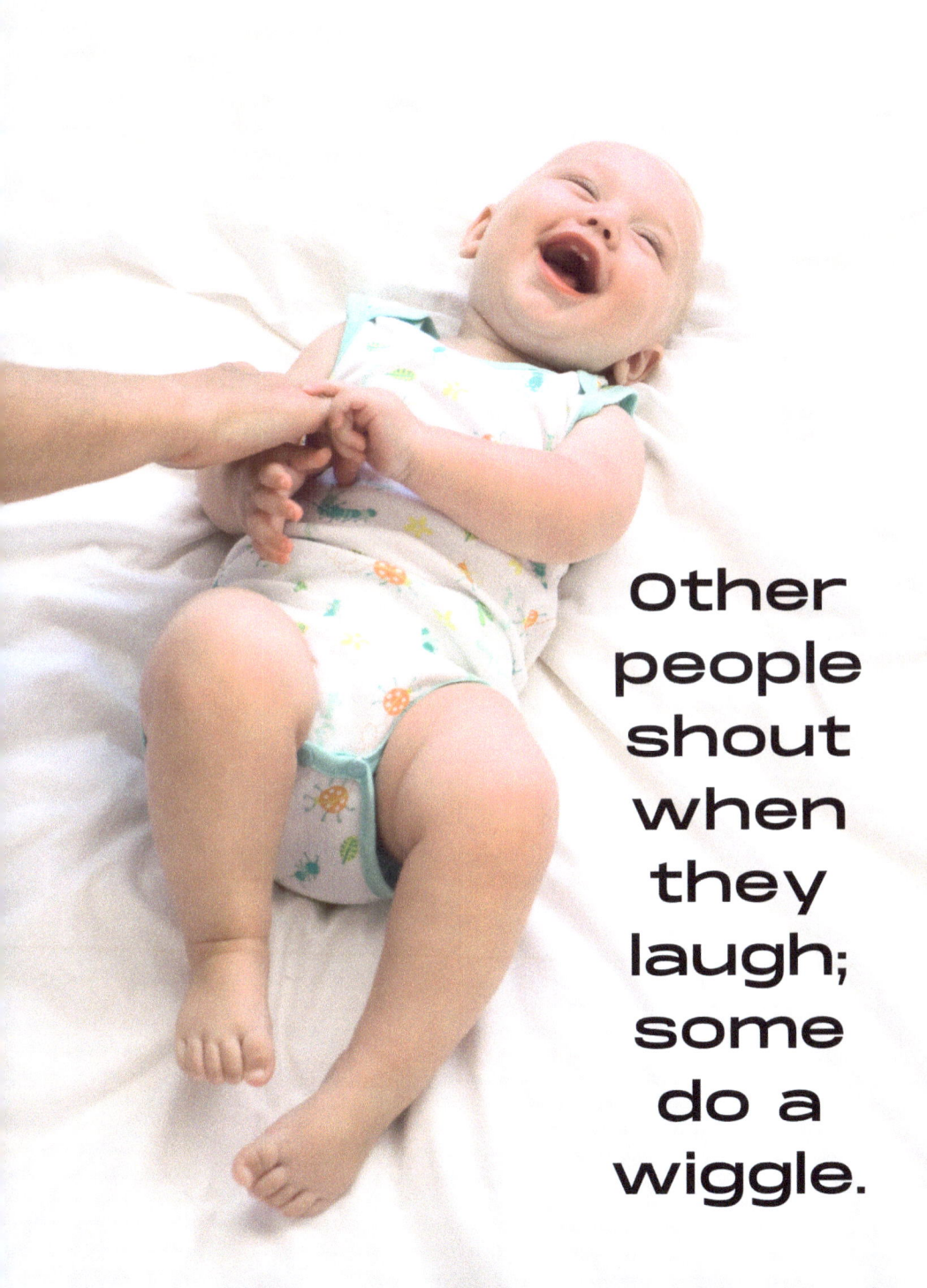

Other people shout when they laugh; some do a wiggle.

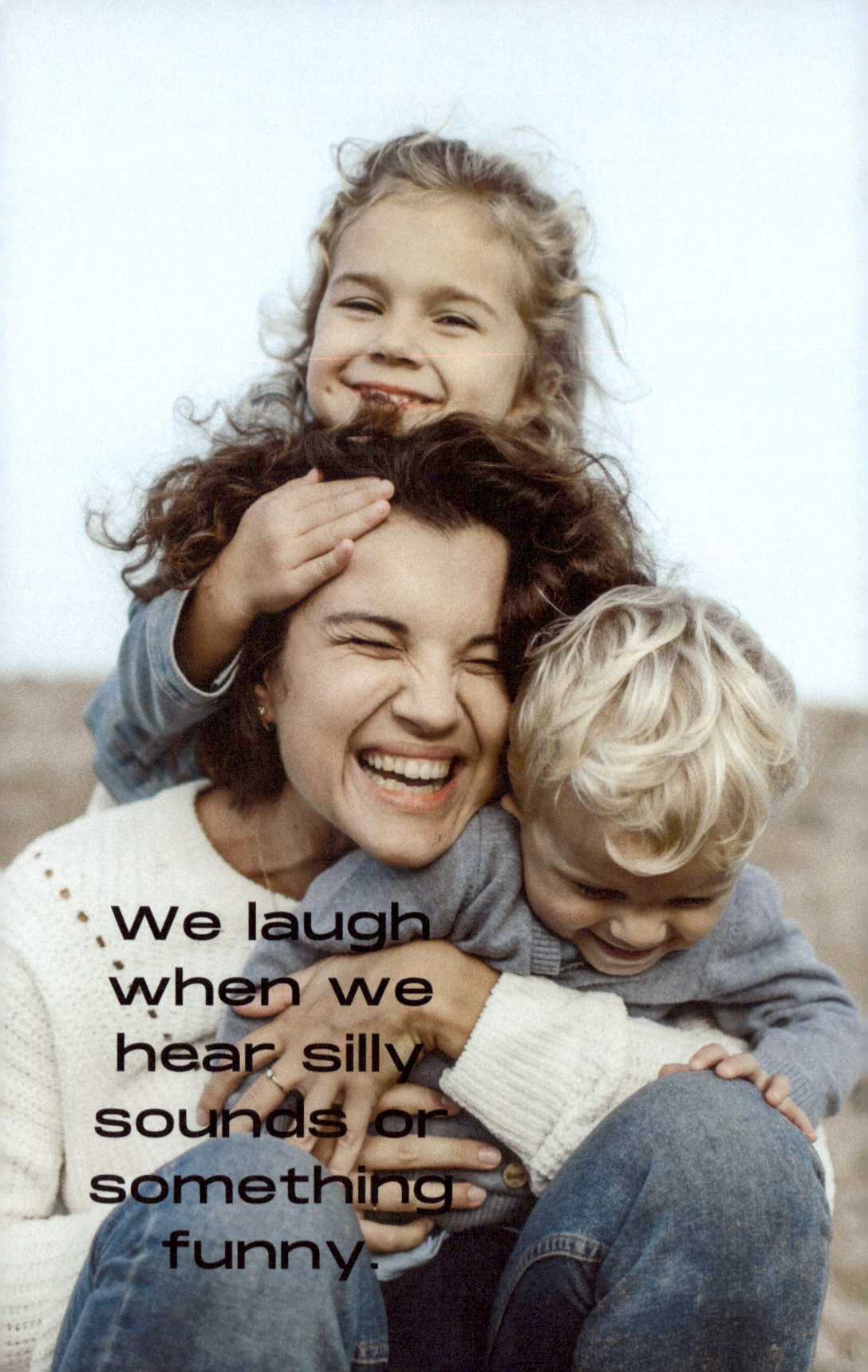

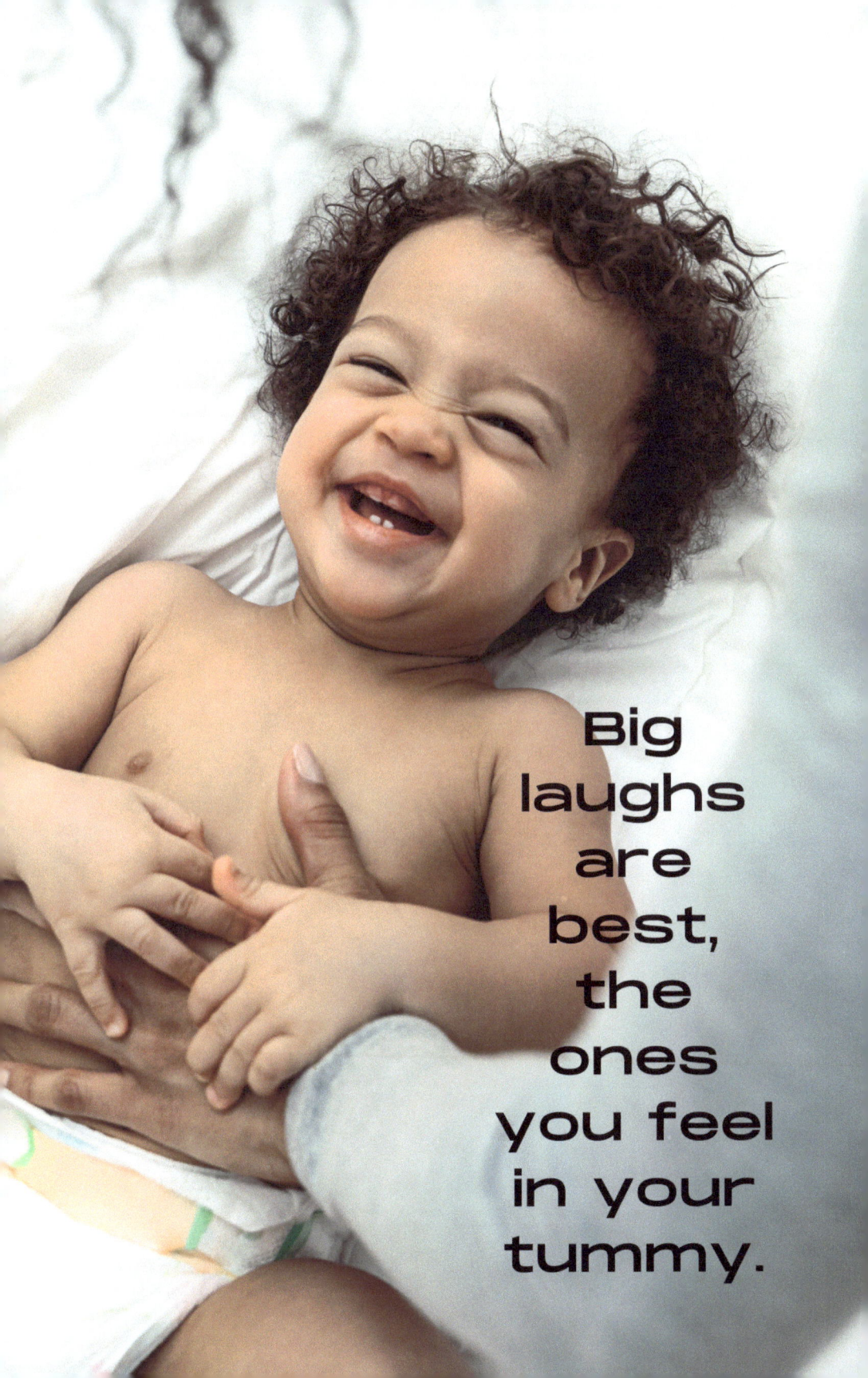

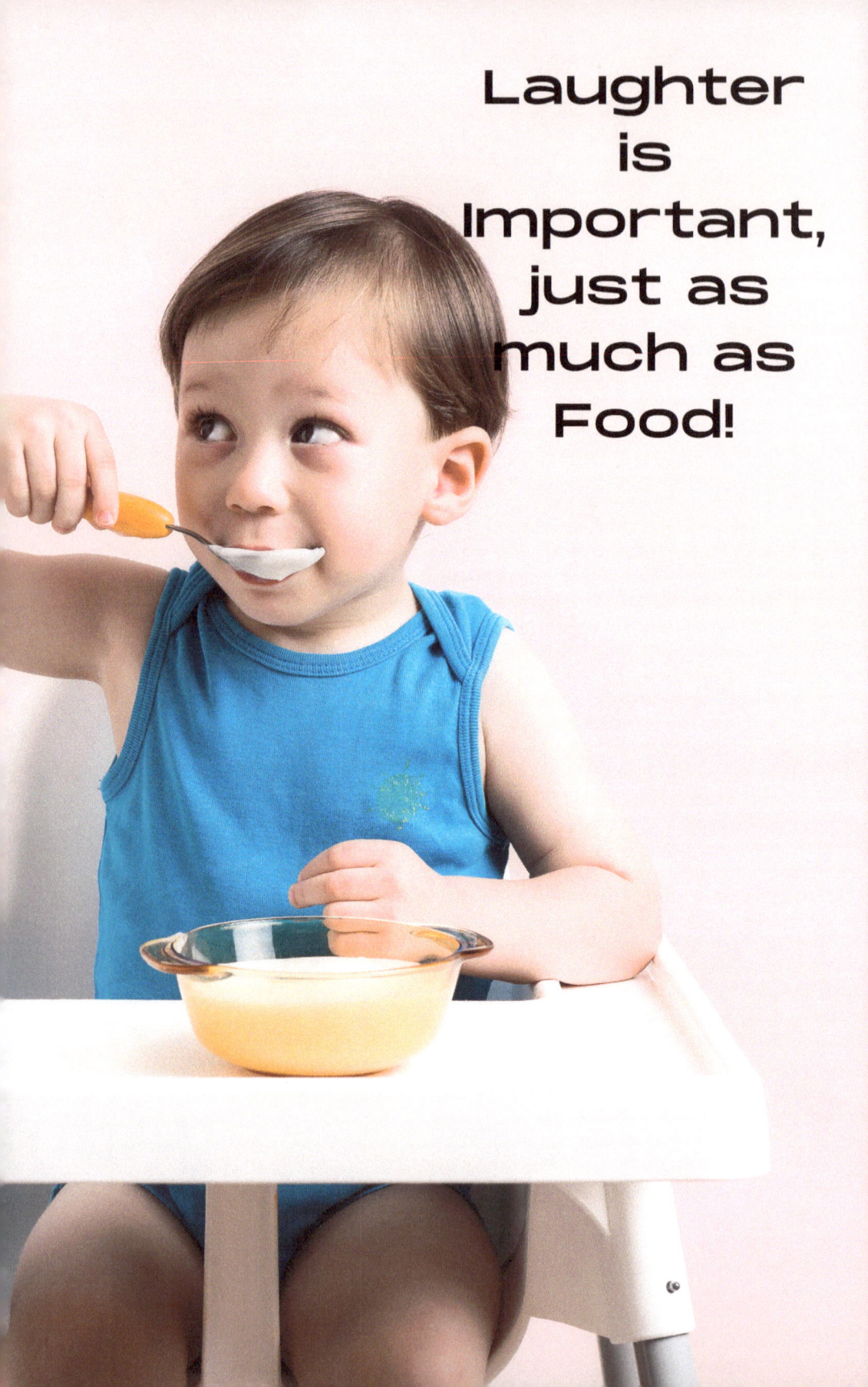

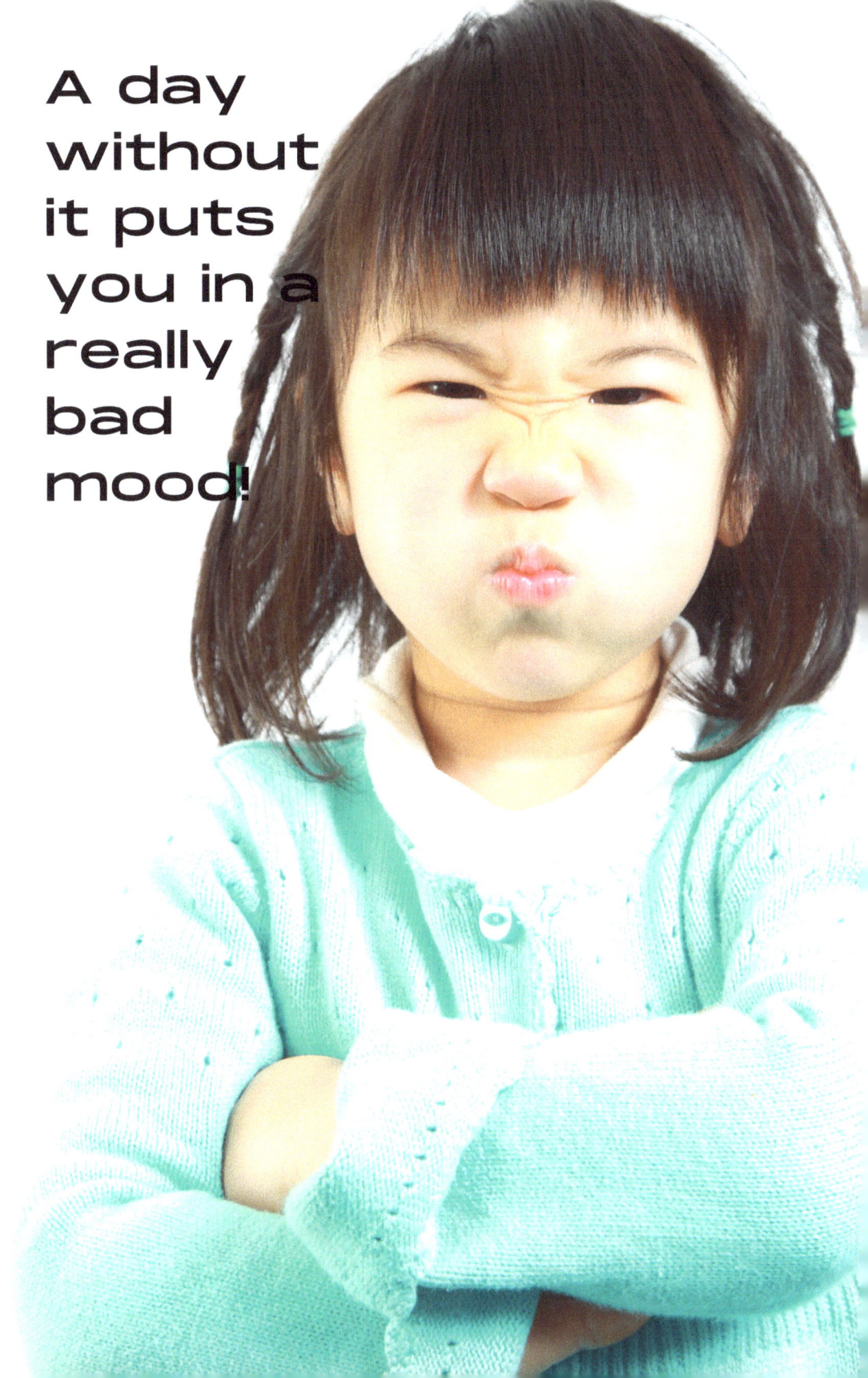

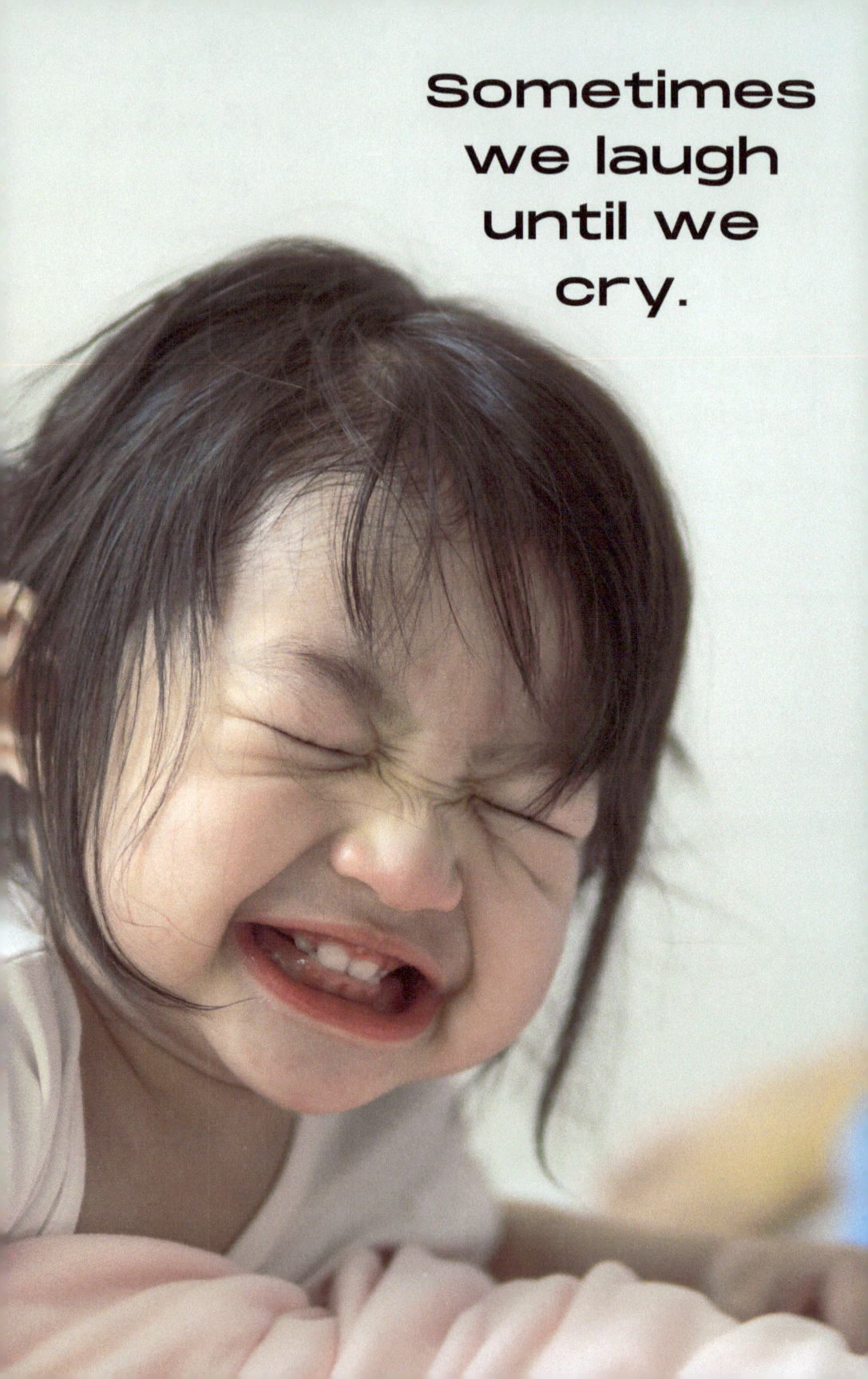

Sometimes we laugh until we cry.

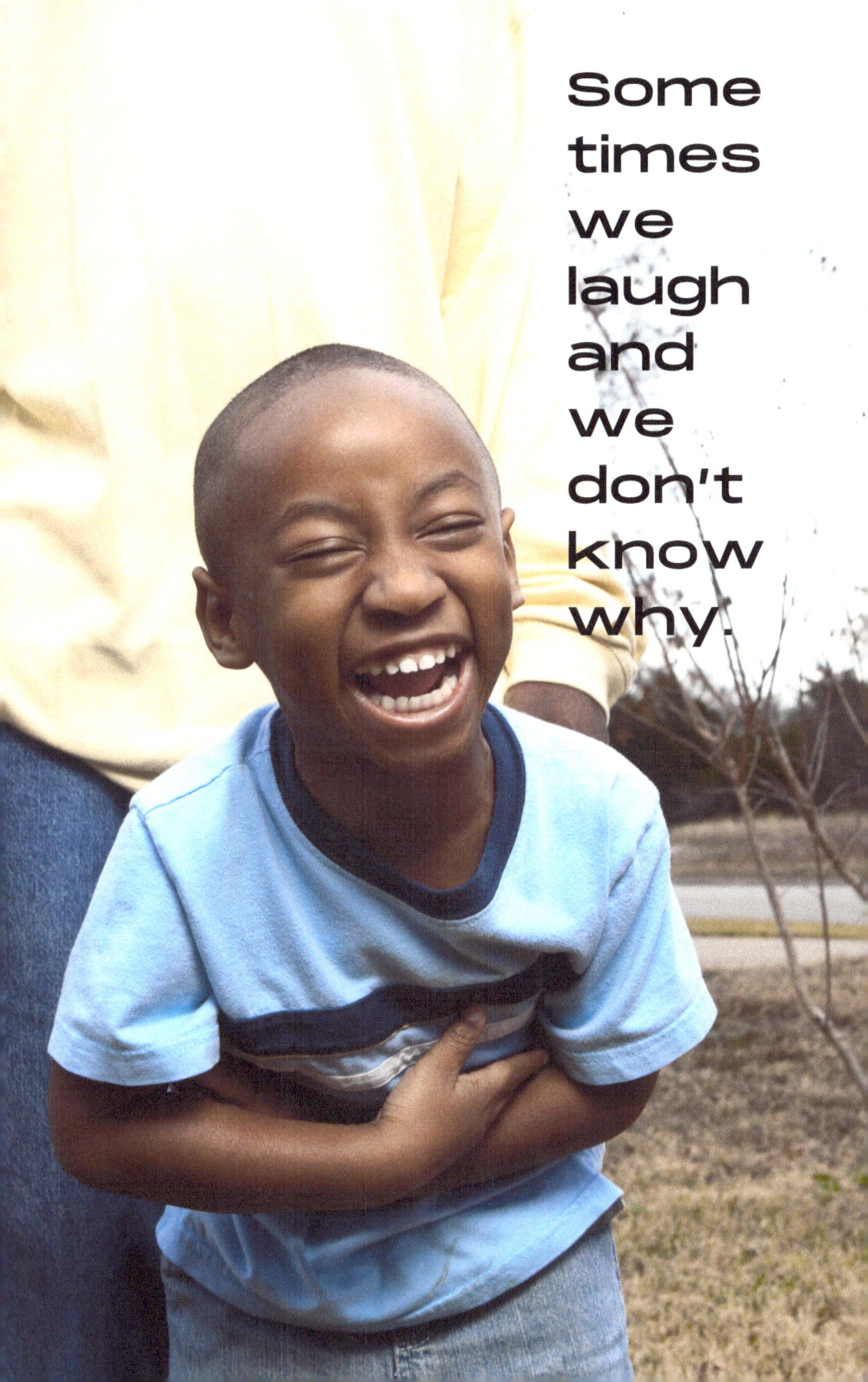

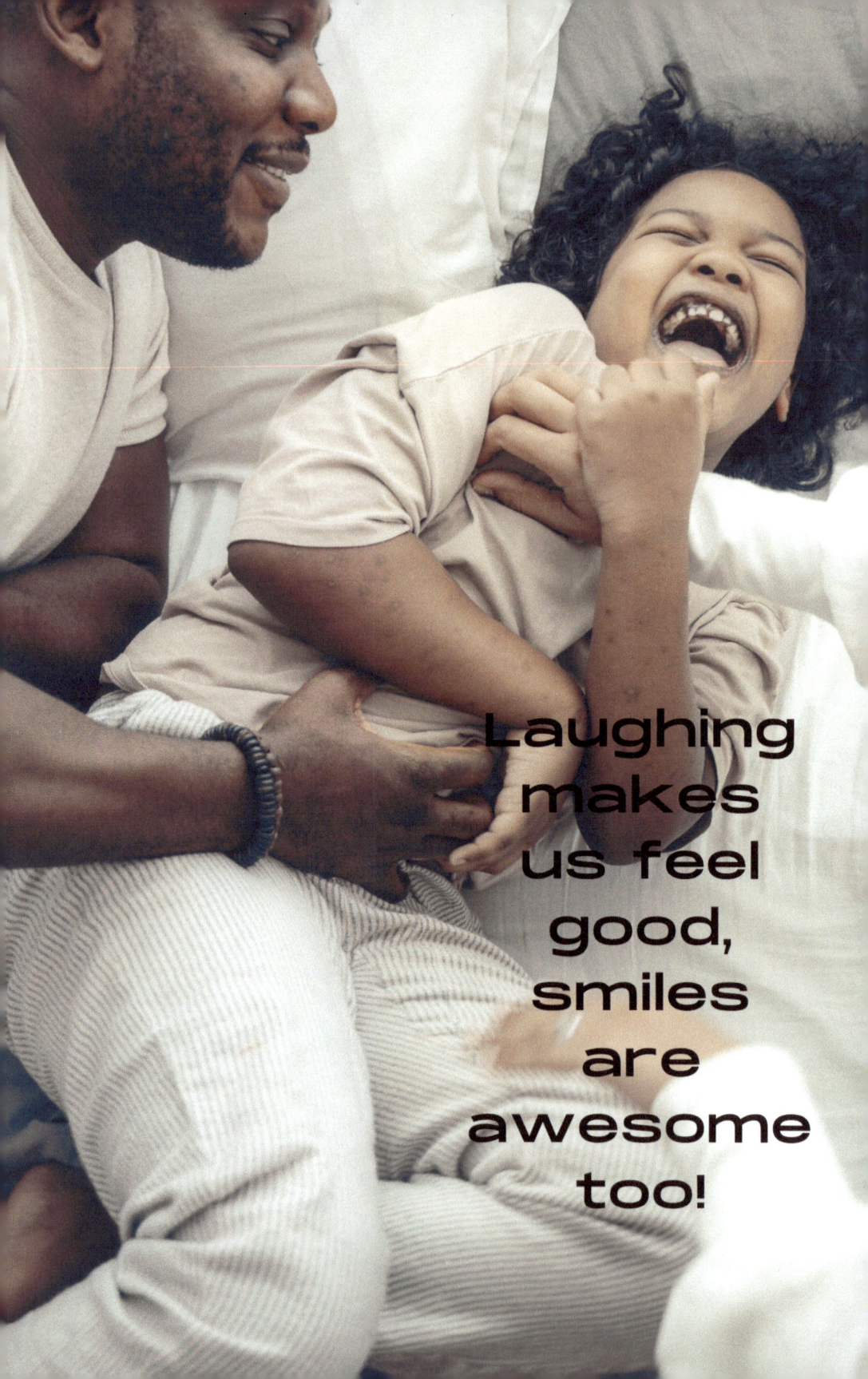

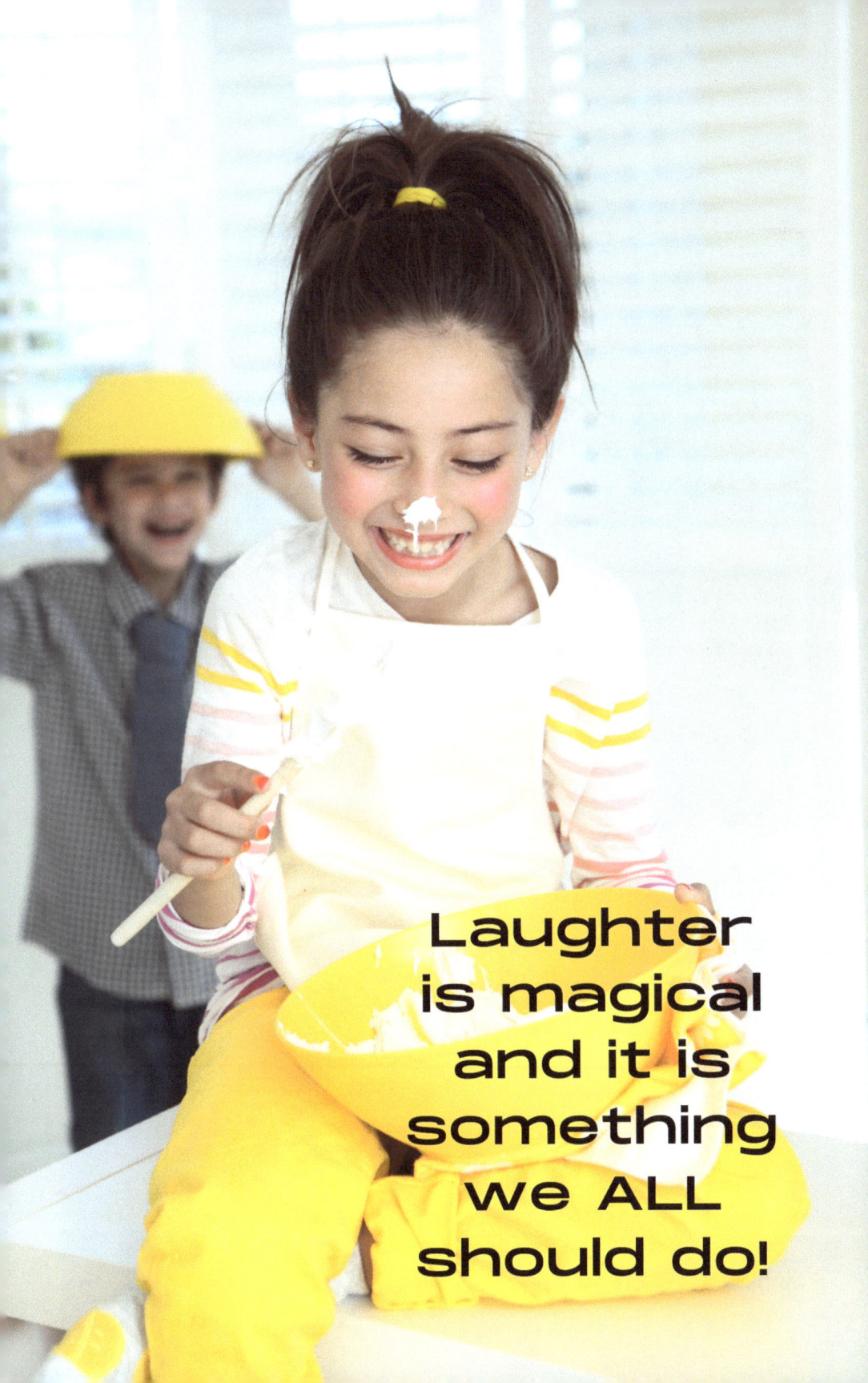

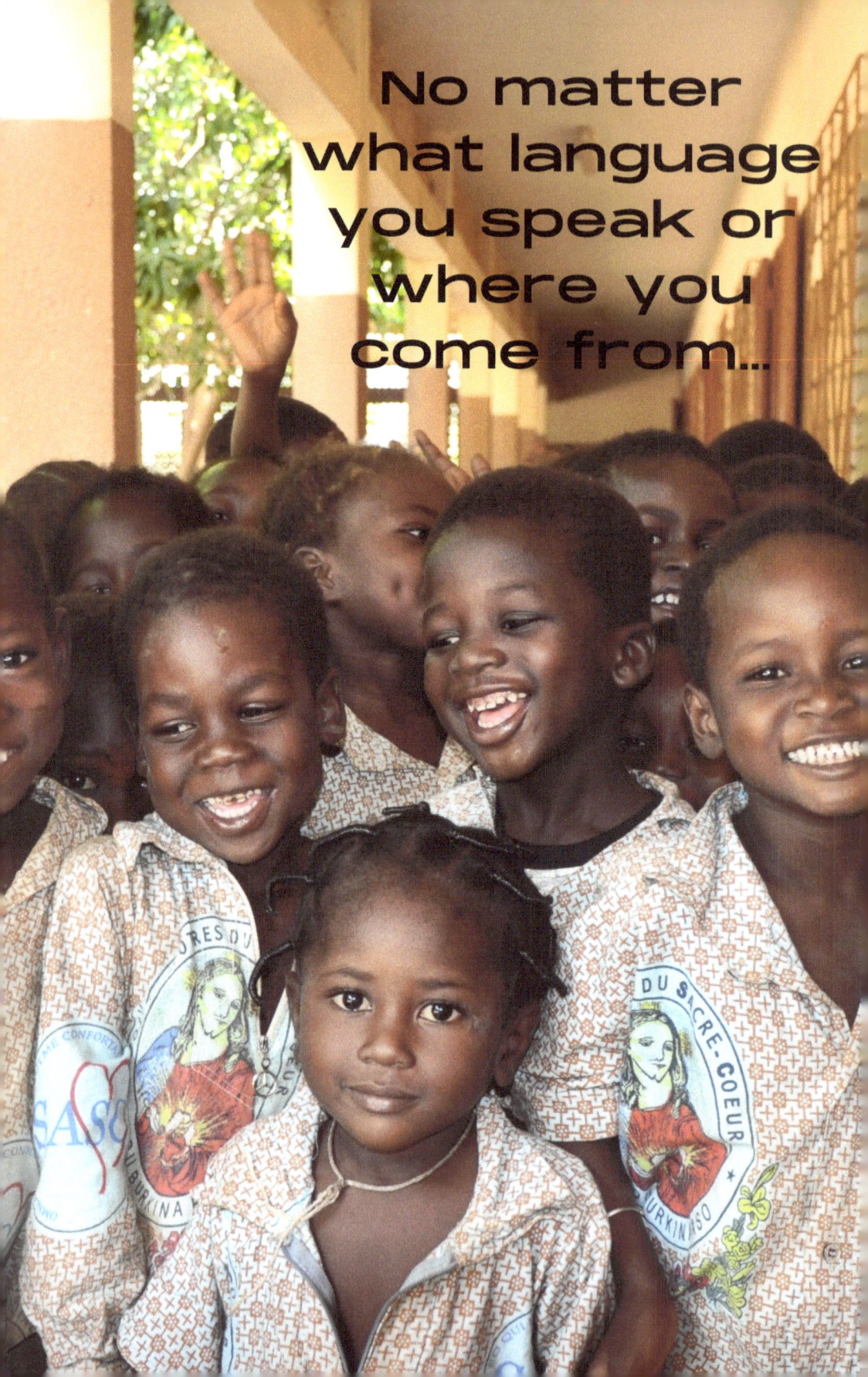

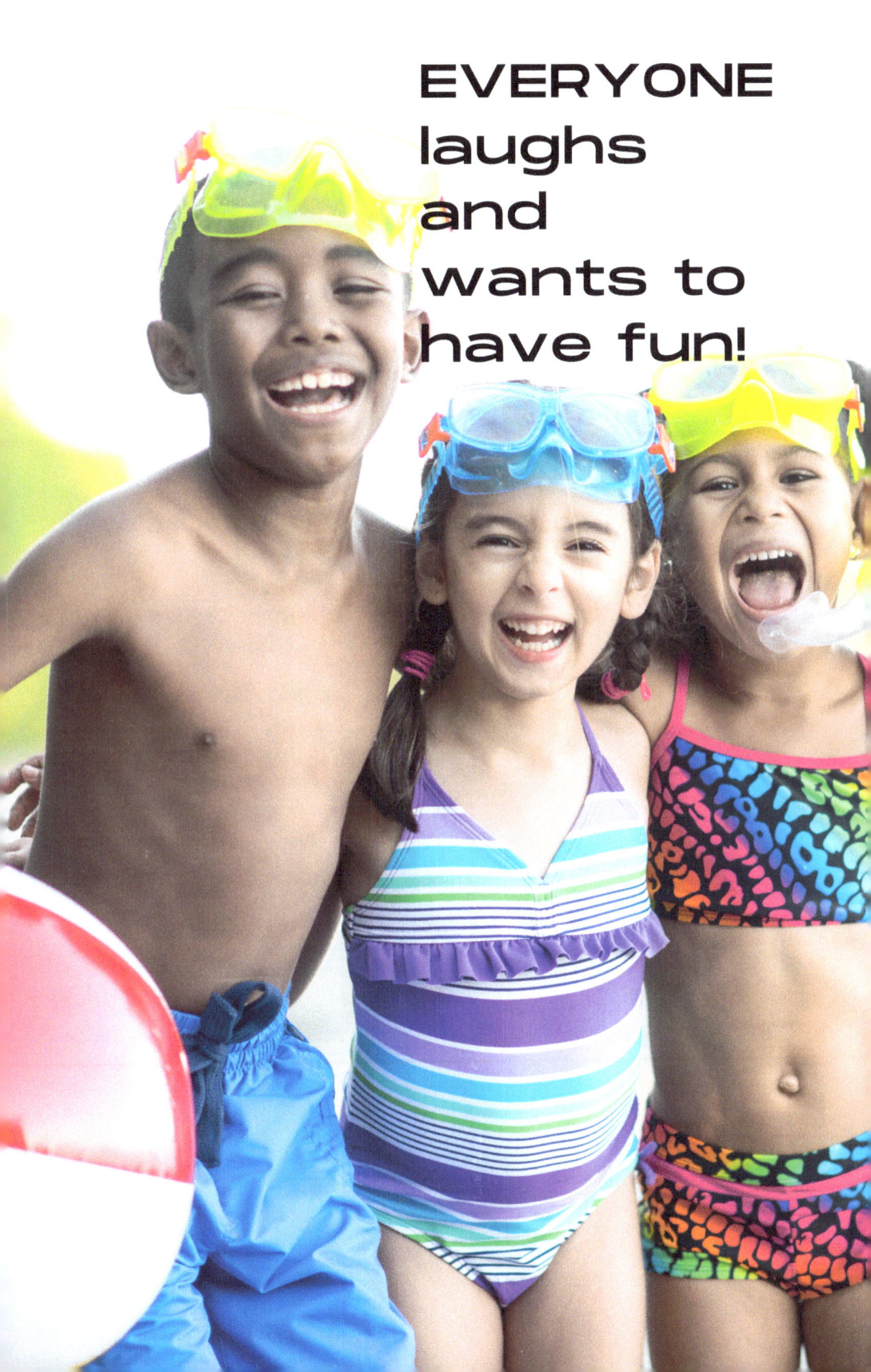

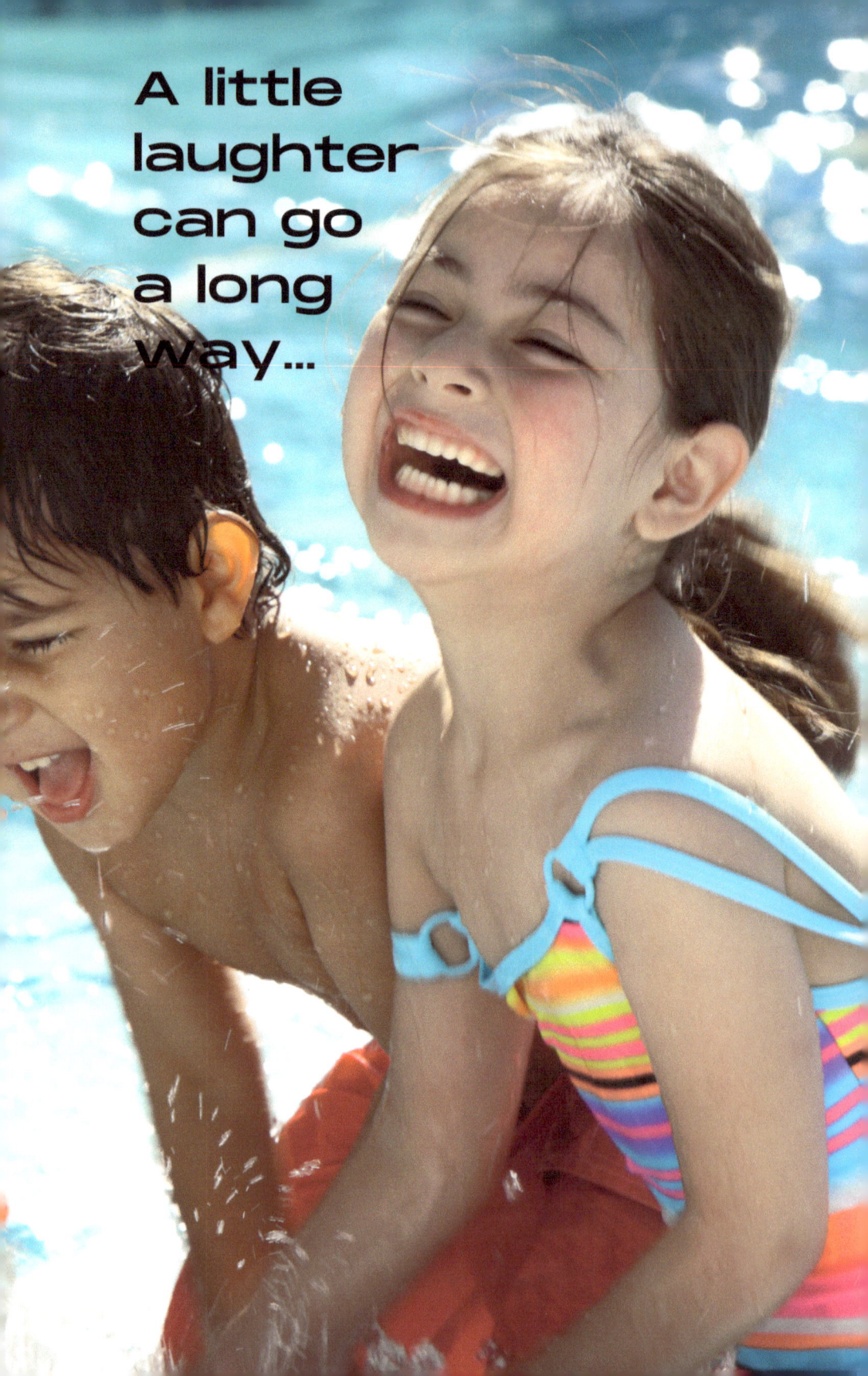

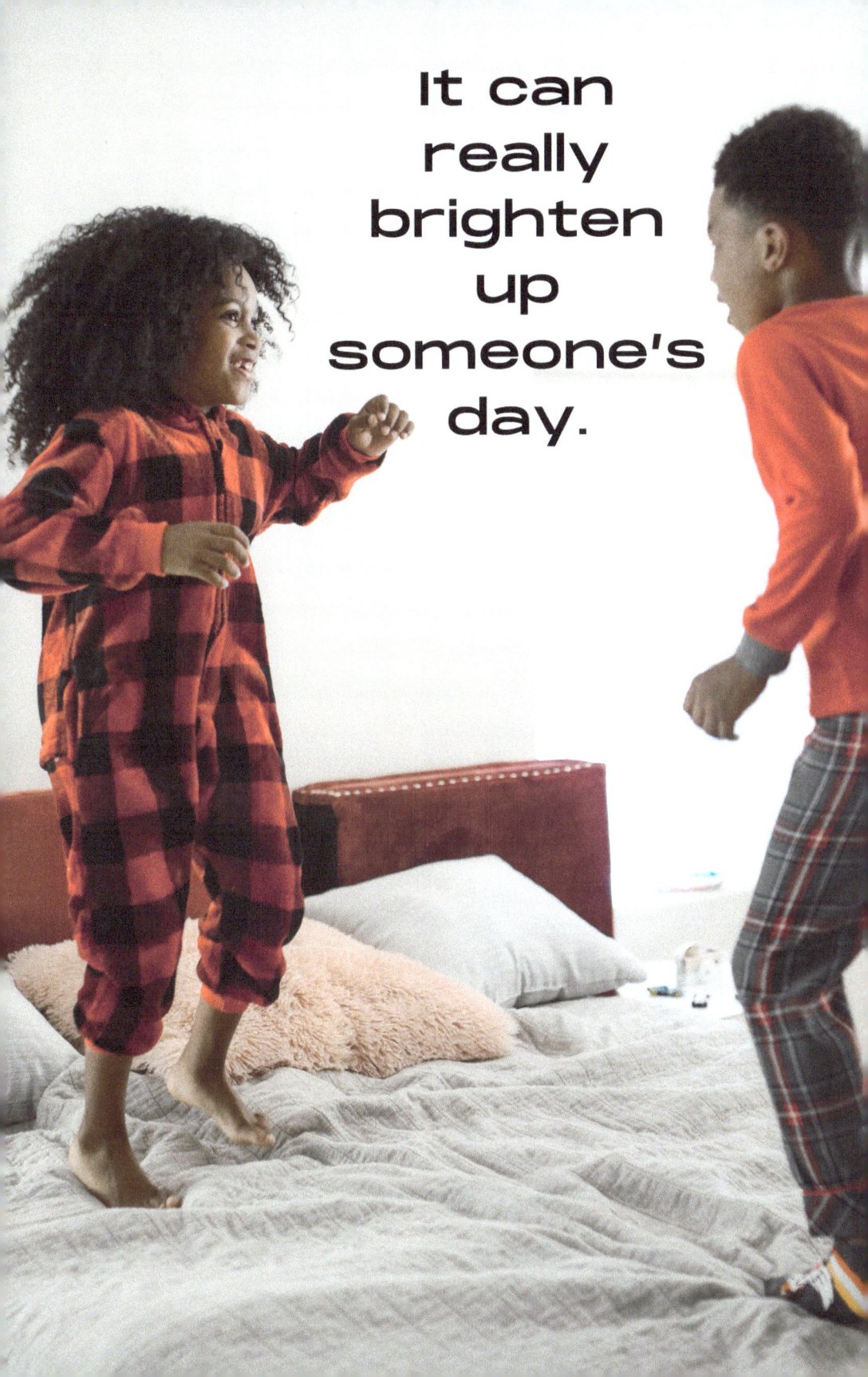

So, If you're feeling down the best thing you can do...

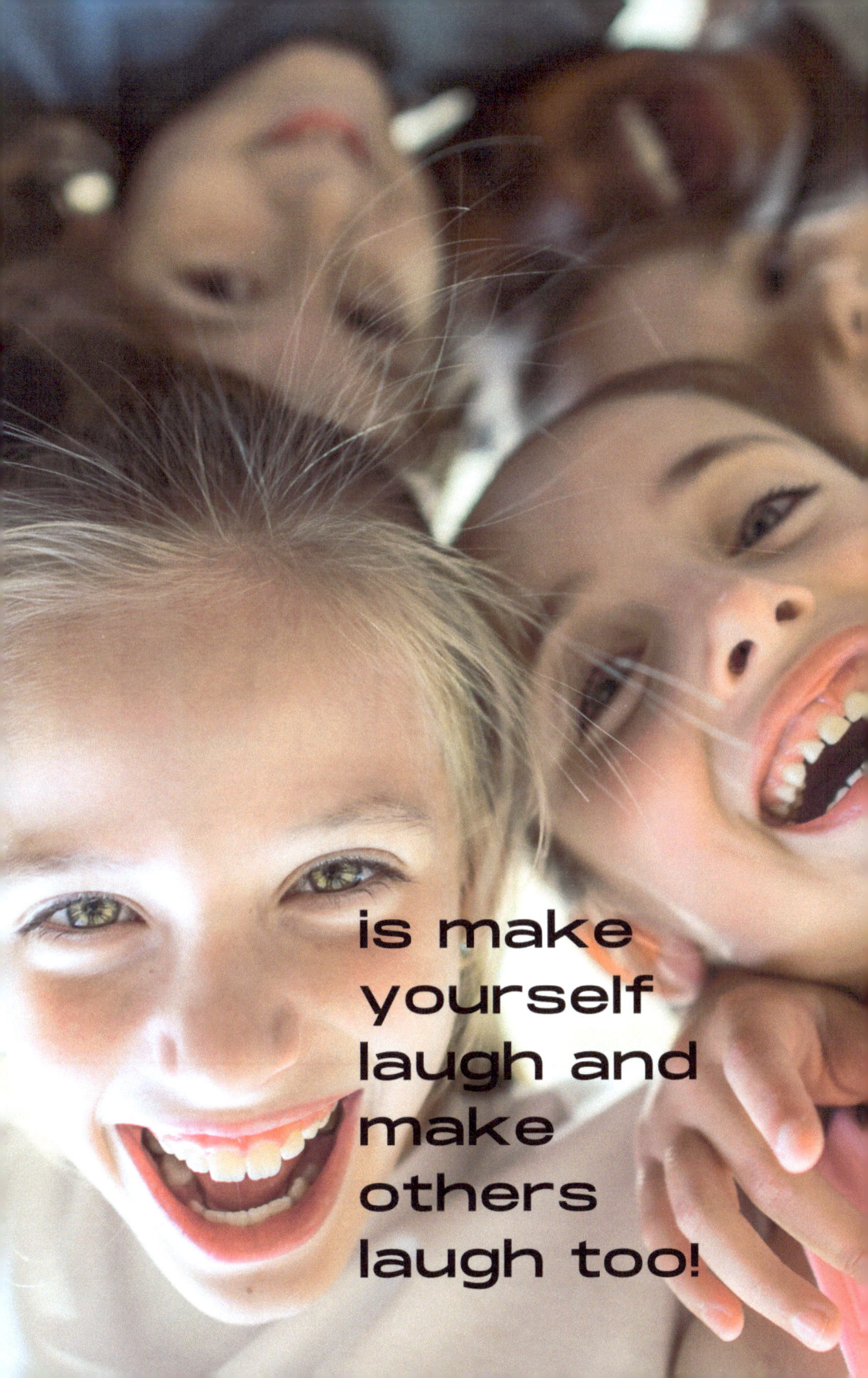

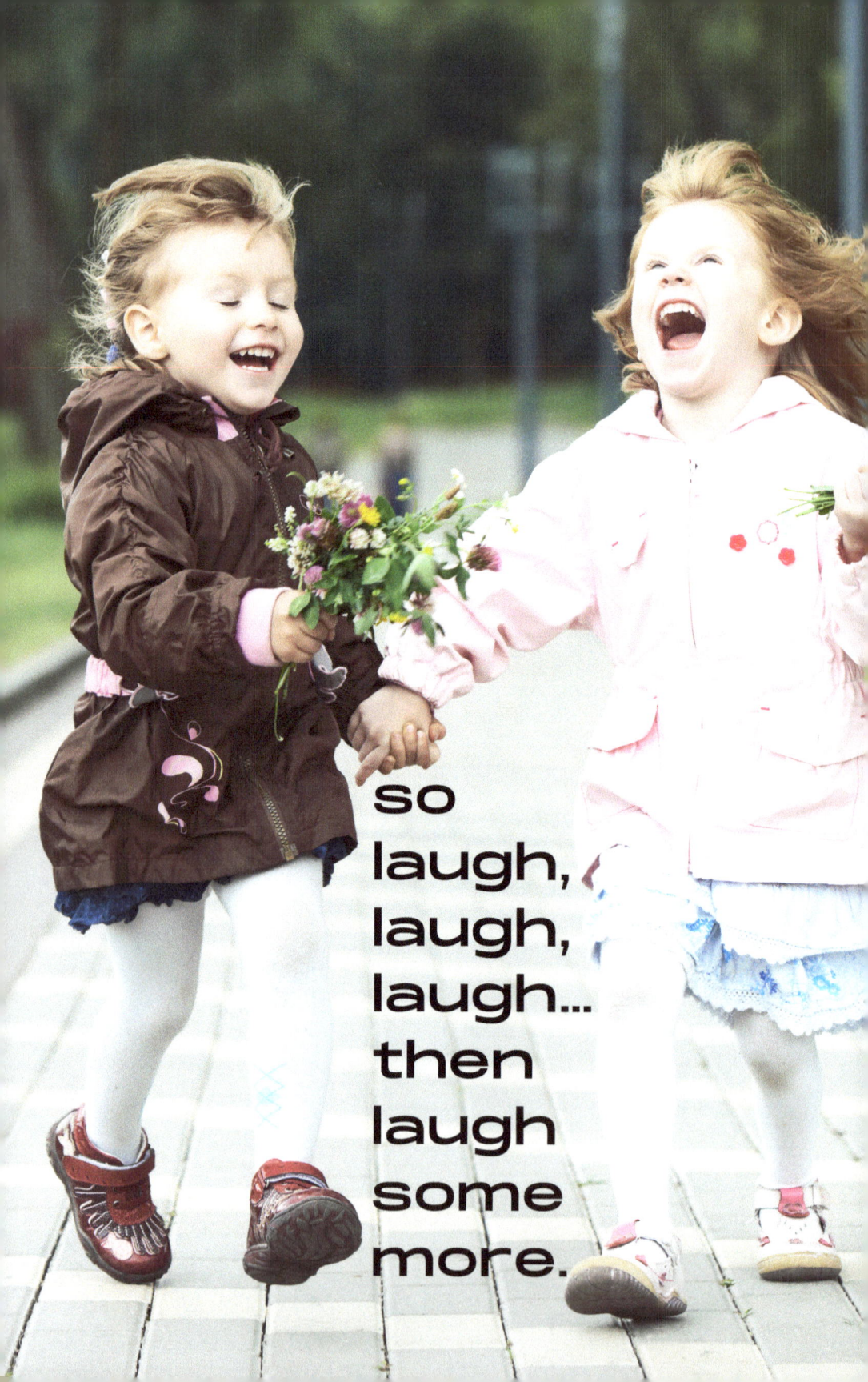

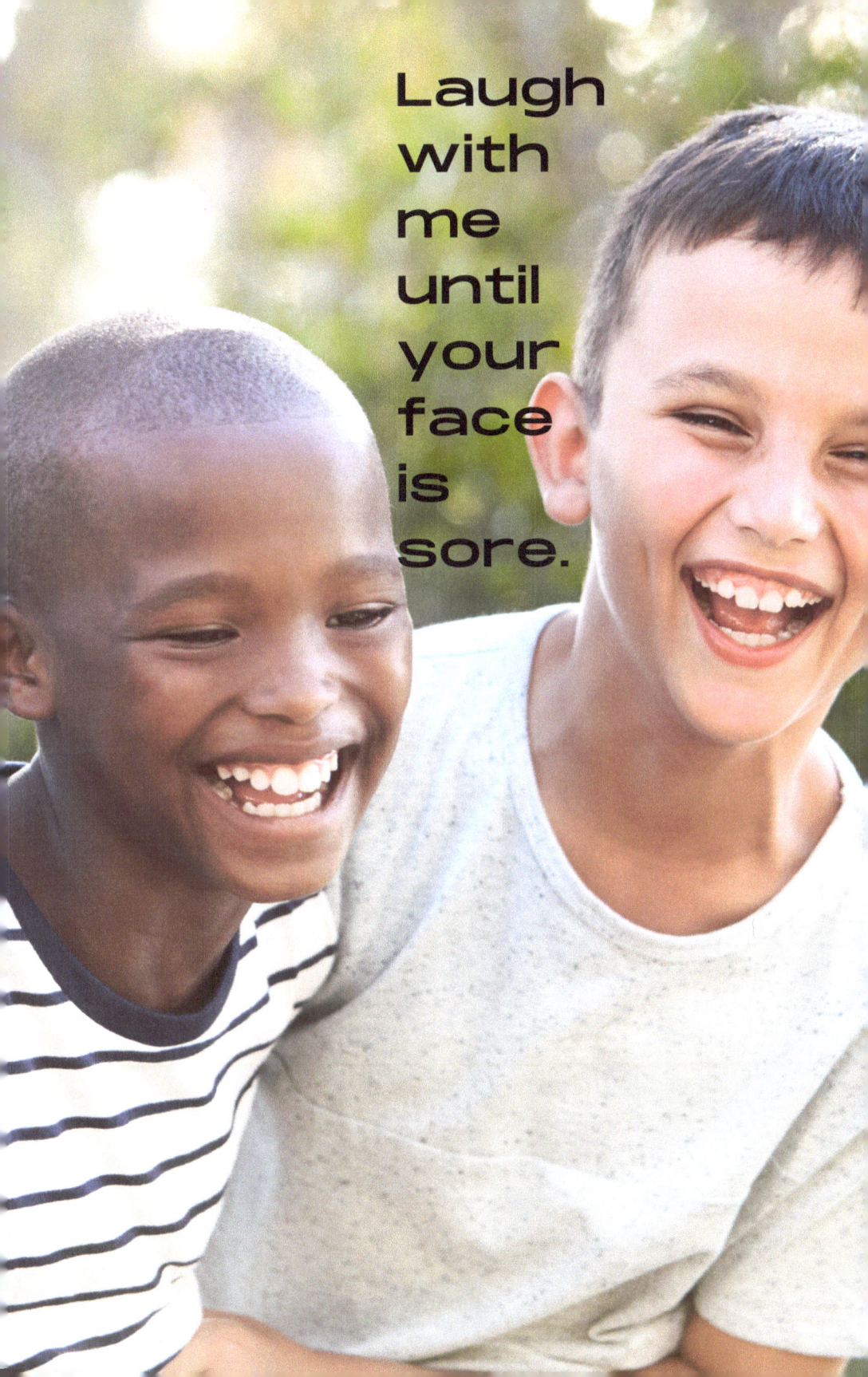

Laugh with me until your face is sore.

I Love to laugh, smile and play

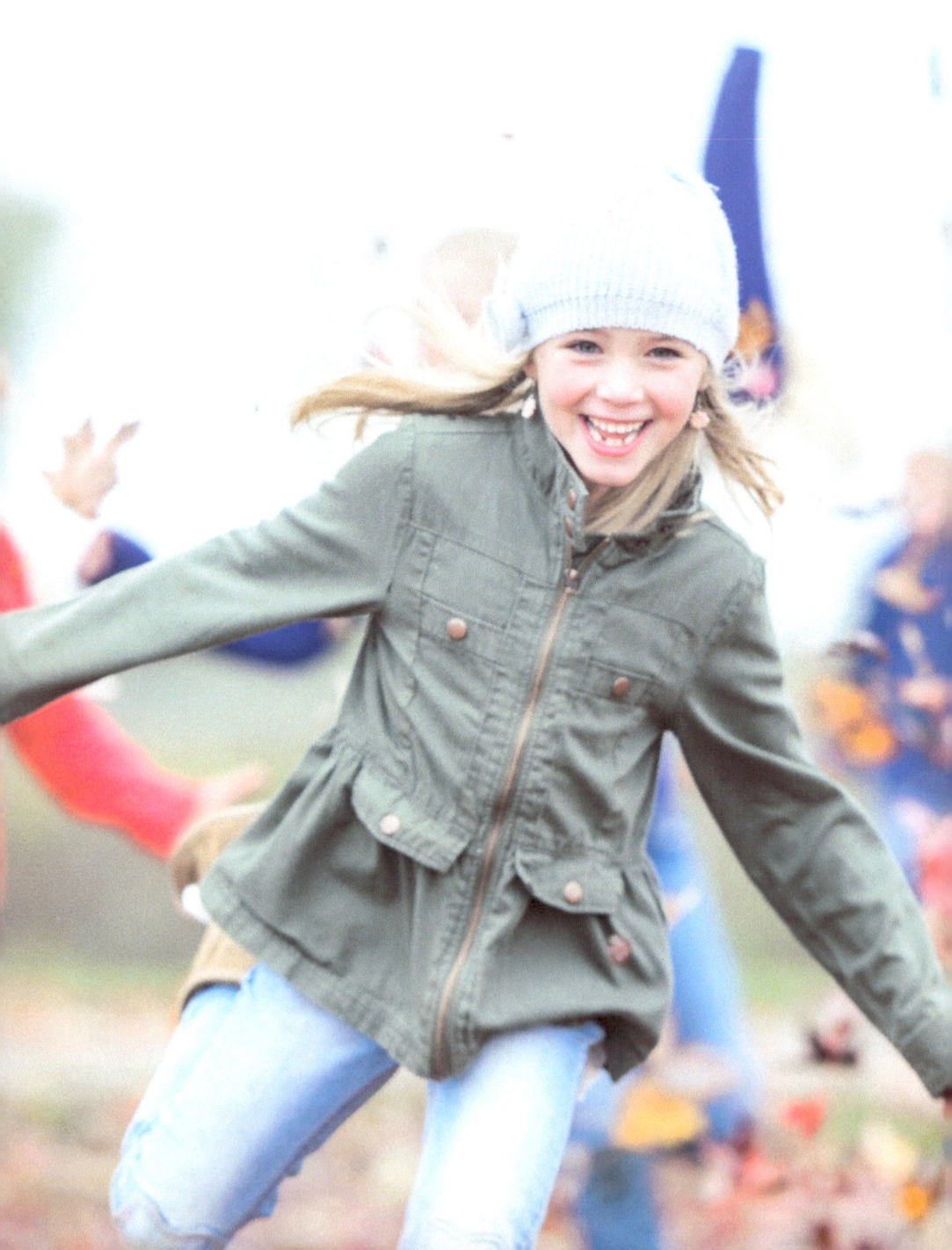

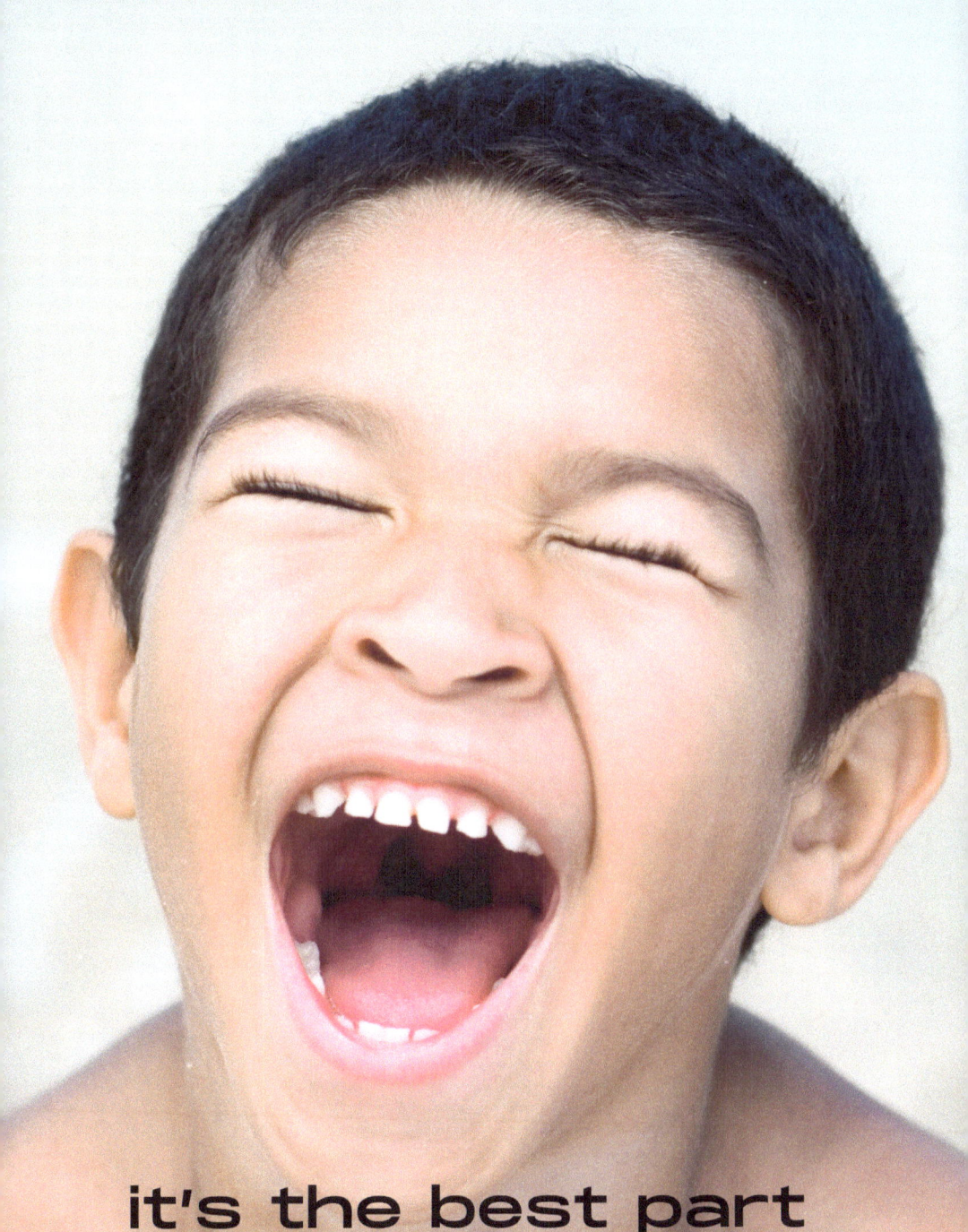

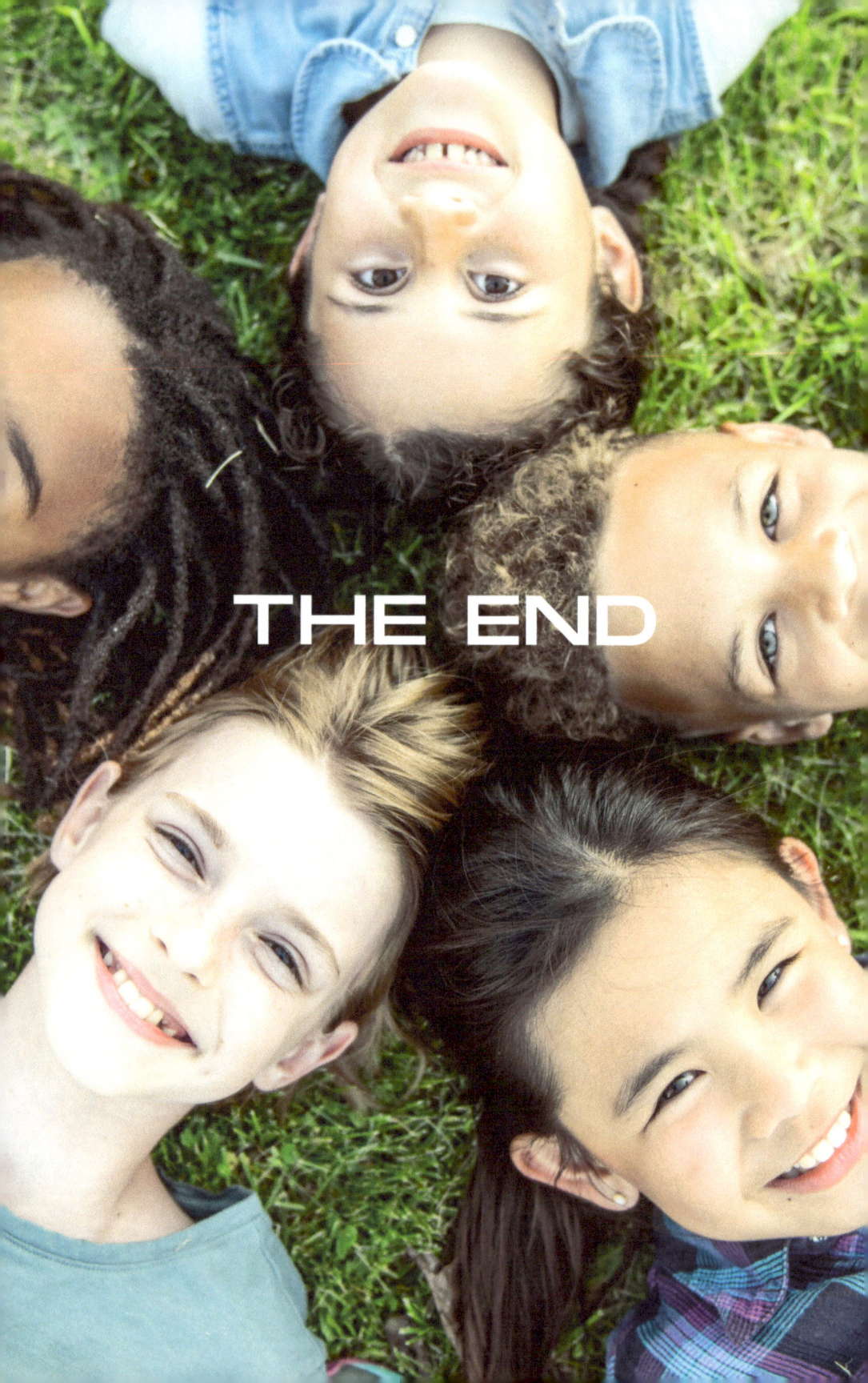

www.ingramcontent.com/pod-product-compliance
Lightning Source LLC
Chambersburg PA
CBHW040302220526
45473CB00002B/558